Let The Ends Spill Over Your Lips

A bedtime story
for those without a bedtime

Poems by Raundi K. Moore-Kondo

ISBN-13: 978-0615857268
For The Love Of Words
949.939.6029
66 WILD HORSE LOOP
RANCHO SANTA MARGARITA, CA 92688

ISBN-10:0615857264

To all of my enablers—

Let The Ends Spill Over Your Lips

If I Had Known You Were Coming

We Could Have Been Hot Like Girl-On-Girl

The Malibu Rum Barbie Interventions

Getting Our Affairs In Orbit

Digging You Up And Holding You Again

IF I HAD KNOWN
YOU WERE COMING

Glossolalia

The dream woke my parents
from their deep, hopeless sleep.
They did not recognize any of the words
coming from my crib.

This was not my mother's tongue.
This was the language of Our Father.

They tried to understand the prophecy that spilled
so effortlessly from my three year-old lips.

From that day on they feared plagues of locusts
might pour from my ears.

They prayed I would build pyramids in the backyard.
That I'd befriend the lost and the lepers.
That the blind would need me to see.

Water could turn into wine, walkway, or holy smoke
in the hands my mother taught me to clasp together.
The ones my father couldn't ever find a reason to slap.

I was proof that whales could swallow us,
but heaven hadn't abandoned us.

They waited for me to dry the flood
and raise their loved ones from the dead.
To feed the sick and heal the hungry.

I haven't accomplished any of it, yet.
I tried to tell them it was only baby talk,
the language of God that we all forget how to speak.

Cake

I measure the flour in secret
by level teaspoonfuls.
I could never tell you exactly how many—
mostly because I don't know.

The sugar to butter ratio
is dependent on the position of the sun
in relation to my favorite of Jupiter's moons.

The 13 eggs must come
from 12 different chickens,
of 11 different species—
and all raised on Mr. Rogers' farm
in the Neighborhood of Make Believe.

The yolks are driven around the park
with the radio on and the windows down,
so they can get a breath of fresh air.

The whites are folded via Buddhist Monk telekinesis.

The milk comes from cows who graze on the grassy
hillsides of Goleta—
overlooking 250-degrees of big blue sea.
I am told they have spent every night
of their lives in a heated barn built by Masons
and are serenaded by Nat King Cole
on vinyl that once belonged to Dick Clark.

The vanilla beans are grown in Bob Dylan's
basement and are read love poems until sunrise.

Virgin surfers from Salt Lake pray
over the pinch of salt.

The pans come directly from Area 51,
and the oven is set to Zen.

The cake is cooled on an open windowsill
and watched over by Aunt Bea.

If I had known you were coming
I would have baked you this cake.
I am sorry to say that all I have is a can
of store bought frosting and a broken plastic spoon.

I hope you'll stay.

Sandbox Sweet-talk

It was sticky. All soft vowels
and spittle-laden consonants.
Lots of squeals and some spontaneous alliteration.

You sang songs about trains
and made jokes about your balls
that I only pretended to understand.

The way you burned-out on three wheels
told me that you were the kind of boy who rebelled
against bedtime rituals, green vegetables,
and parental advisory warnings.

Despite one or two mild tantrums, I was wet riveted
by your helicopter and motorcycle impersonations.

You showed me how far cheesy goldfish could fly,
and that boys are better than girls because they can pee
in bushes without getting their socks wet.

Your devil-may-care juice box squeezes and roly-poly
autopsies both impressed and frightened me.
You enjoyed a little sand in my peanut butter sandwich
while explaining about your pet T-Rex.
No, you weren't scared—
he was trained and only ate girls.

You drove bulldozers and stolen police cars.
You ran Barbie down and buried her alive.
Then ate all the broken bits of sidewalk chalk
and made my last piece soggy by sucking
on it like a cigarette.

The first time you called me *baby*

it was because I couldn't see smoke.

You got kinda quiet after skinning your knee.
Then yelled about hating jump ropes, your neighbors
black dog with the spiked collar, and *babies*,
"Every Goddamned last one of 'em!"

You wished your dad wouldn't ever come home
and were especially suspicious of how big the bulge
in your mama's belly was getting.

I confided that blowing bubbles had become boring
both in swim class and in the bathtub.
I liked chocolate milk, frilly slips,
and the taste of pink Play-Doh best.

That's when you lifted my dress.
After seeing my panties, you dumped
out my Cheerios for the pigeons
and smeared boogers in my hair.

When your back was turned
and you were in line for the swings
I hit you over the head with your plastic-shovel.
God, how you cried.
I said something cute, like—
who's the baby now?

Later that day after untying my laces
and right before shoving me backward
down the dark tunnel of the twisty slide,
you kissed me hard.
I can clearly recall the serrated edges
of both your bottom teeth and the first taste
of my own blood on someone else's lips.

The Pre-History Of Us

We dripped from adjacent tile shingles of a roof,
    in precise unison.
Falling 9.8 meters per second, per second,
    just like everyone else.
Mosh pit choreography was imbedded
    in our chemical make-up.
We were born to slam dance, pop, lock,
    and improvise.
Jesus promised us that his father had a sacred plan
    for every drop.
Buddha trusted that each glob of molecules
    would find its purpose.
Mohammad praised our sacred path
    before we ever left the sky.
God himself guaranteed divine justice
    and that nothing was blind.
Einstein smiled at our chaos, stuck his tongue out
    at our Galapagos and Darwin winked back.
Shakespeare laughed and cried, and laughed.
    Then wrote and wrote and wrote about us.
We were the birth of tragic comedy
    and the death of reality T.V.
Coltrane offered free stardust rides
    all day and night until,
Nirvana formed, and we started taking too much
    Cobain in our coffee.
When our surface tension was breached by asphalt
    we become one with the puddle.
Our individuality embraced dementia like your hand
    wrapped around single malt.
The shadows on the cave walls lost
    all of their novelty.
Kevorkian's black boot attempted to liberate us
    from our low-lying bed.

We couldn't get up because Jung was still telling
        fairy tales. But we still couldn't sleep.
At least not until anonymous futility became something
        worth suckling on.
We are told this is peace. Like our skin,
        I do not know where mine ends or yours begins.

Birthday Litany

for Billy Collins

I am the icing and the cake.
You are the fork and the plate,
the ice cream and the spoon,
the pointed hats,
and whistling party flavors.

You are the syrup-sweet punch,
rainbow sprinkles,
and marshmallow fluff
sucked from my hair.

You are not however
the balloons high on helium
or the twisted streamers strung low.

It is possible you are the wax,
and the wick,
whose fire
can be snuffed
with a blow, a tug, and a lick.

But you are not the wish on my lips
or the smoke scented air—
there is no way you are the smoke scented air.

Nor are you the spinning bottle.

It might interest you to know that I am the spinning bottle.

And, the 7 minutes in heaven.
The crystal sugar lips
and the pink-stained tongue.

You are the lock on the door,
the dark in the room,
and the sticky fingers.

I Never Dreamed You'd be My Type

On the day it rained you offered me the cleanest corner
of your refugee camp t-shirt to wipe ashes from my eyes.
The dead pigeon at our feet shuddered slightly
before maggots burst from its distended belly.

You complimented my strong gut,
the whiteness of my teeth,
and pretended not to notice the bloodstains
on my hands and knees.

Your eyes were still proud.
I could tell you wouldn't ever try to rape me.
I wouldn't ever have to try to kill you.

I learned to read your shoulder language
when you spoke of your neighbor's dog,
and his broken neck.

You only nodded when I told you how my mother died
believing she was being taken with the rapture.

I was glad I had used what was left of the rabbit entrails
to add a little color to my lips and cheeks,
because you brought me wild carrots and white mushrooms
that grew inside the cemetery between our streets.

That's when I knew I would marry you.

When the fish decayed on the shore,
I wondered if you still loved me.

The fields burn wild.
I only think of when I will see you again.

The wells have been poisoned.
I daydream of your hand on the small of my back.

My youngest brother died this morning.
I pretend to make a bed for us in your father's house.

I want you to know that I am singing
as I pick flees from my sister's hair, and I smile.

Should I Warn You About The Scars?

I could describe them.
Their general vicinity, their severity,
and little of their history.

Try to get you to fall prematurely
in love with every cure that hasn't killed me.

I've run my hands across the traces of former injuries,
caressed the raised marks of tissue over-proliferation,
and fingered the depth of each recession
like a new lover might.

Is it even possible to soften the blow to your mind?
If only to prolong the inevitabilities,
I could just keep quiet,
turn off the lights,
and hope you proceed without noticing anything
that feels especially unsightly.

But I can't help imagining your hand
stuttering across my stomach,
backing-up and making a second pass
as if to say—
Wait… What the hell was that?

I'm not sure how to prepare your mind's eye
for all the hypertrophic sculpture
and the atrophic blueprints of neglect.

Un-planned, un-plotted wannabe tattoos
from growth spurts, submarine rocks, forked tongues,
pregnant pauses, and numerous hard-on collisions
with one poorly-positioned nightstand.

I've searched for someone to blame only to find
all were made possible by my errors in judgment:
wandering in the dark,
moving too fast,
braking too hard,
asking the wrong questions
or just plain not paying enough attention.

They are each reminders of the near misses.
All those end over end bicycle stunts.
All the times I've survived well enough to walk away.

I try not to refer to all of my damages
as permanent, since some will fade with time.
Yet, they amount to pretty much the same thing—proof
that I can endure a certain amount of brutality.

As a survivor standing in your point blank range
I can only hope these scars have prepared me for you.

The Donut Shop

It had become our sanctuary. The hard backed booths felt a lot like church pews. They were always just uncomfortable enough to make certain kinds of confessions come easy. Our elbows stabbed the sugar-stained, pink, Formica tabletop in search of the least sticky spots. In that way, it felt a little like home.

I only ever drank the coffee, and you liked the lukewarmness of the water fountain. All six feet, two inches of you insisted on using the stepstool so you could tower over the spout. You said it was because you liked drinking water best from the backside, when it was falling upside down. To me, it was another Freudian slip that indicated your desire to use everything at once whether you needed it or not.

The Donut shop was always open after the clubs closed and our parties went postal. The smell of rising yeast and rainbow sprinkles made us feel like we could grow younger, happier versions of ourselves. Unlike the bars, where you made suicide-pacts with me and your short-term, memory loss. You never knew or cared that I always stayed sober enough to recall everything you said.

Tonight you wanted to marry your ex-girlfriend, so you could finally grow up and fill that monster of a body with a larger version of yourself. You thought that would mean less room for empty bottles and obscenities to rattle around. You ordered a dozen donuts as a party for courage. You told, Jesus, the night manager to surprise you and to "mix it up". Your only stipulation was that they all had to have holes.

You proclaimed that buying in bulk was your first and next step toward becoming an adult. I sat in our booth while you practiced slipping donuts on my right ring finger until you found the best fit.

Once the sun came up you would walk to her house with a donut in your pocket. When she answered the door you would drop to one knee and offer her the kind of future that couldn't be planned for.

To me it sounded lame. I imagined all that cake and frosting gumming up your pocket and you holding out a handful of crumbs. I shouldn't have tried to talk you out of it. It was the most honest offer you would ever make. You insisted your plan was brilliant and that she would cry and forgive you for all the nights ahead. I knew her better than that. She wasn't going to like it, but no one listens to reason while dough is frying.

You threw the box against the windowpane. Donuts exploded and bounced along the tabletops and rolled across the confetti linoleum. You were hysterical that none of them would do. You would have to make the perfect ring yourself or you wouldn't marry at all.

What began as peaceful negotiations turned into you threatening to beat up Jesus if he didn't let you behind the counter and teach you how to make the perfect ring. Jesus hung his head, held up his hands in prayer, and then lifted the counter divider. It was the perfect surrender.

Our floury hands dove deep into the elastic-wet of all those future glazed, twists, rings, and holes. Like everything else we stretched the dough as far as it would go. It must have been 15 feet from the back alley to the front door. It sagged in the middle, and we had to drag it across the floor.

We dipped everything in cake batter to be pressure tested by the deep fryer including: a cardboard box of Yoo-hoo, a stapler, a saltshaker, a roll of quarters, and a condom filled with custard cream.

Lastly, your masterpiece ring of golden cake batter was born without pomp or circumstance. The three of us stared at it alone on a monstrous cooling rack; for a moment we all believed that it was special.

It was glazed first, as a preservative of sorts. Cinnamon sugared before the glaze hardened and then frosted in both pink and chocolate icing to form a yin yang symbol. It was lay to rest on a bed of fluffy white coconut, rainbow sprinkled, and lastly given a light dusting of powdered, non-dairy creamer.

Jesus handed you the jelly injector, but you turned it down and said, "What? Are you crazy? This jelly was made for donuts without holes. For God's sake man, this is my engagement ring were talking about. Have you no pride in your work?" Jesus wasn't even shocked when you shoved the engagement ring donut deep into the pocket of your jeans.

We discovered a lot that night. Like maybe that we are better at admiring donuts and marriages than we'd ever be at making them ourselves. That night managers can be paid off in weed. That deep-frying condoms filled with custard cream can make a big fucking mess. And that your words tasted better dipped in whisky than in cinnamon sugar.

It would be 3 hours until the real customers arrived wanting to buy donuts for office meetings and classroom birthday parties. All they would have to choose from were glazed phalli in a variety of sizes and breast-shaped donut holes with a single, pink jimi-nipple adorning each one. Turns out it was Jesus' last night on the job anyway. He was moving to the valley to open a produce stand. He told us how he despised the taste of refined sugar and having to put up with drunks. "Nothing personal," he added. He refused to help another fat lady buy diet soda and powdered-sugar, doughnut breakfasts for her borderline-diabetic kids.

We've been banned from the shop. So now after the bars we sit on the curb inhaling the youth of rising dough and colored sprinkles. It smells a little less hopeful from the street. "I'd kill for a cup of coffee," I say.

Your response, "My one regret is that I didn't steal the step-stool that night we had the place to ourselves."

My Way To Your Heart

I butter your toast.
Spread it out to all four of your imperfect
corners to achieve the ideal toast-to butter-ratio.

Butter will yield to a cold knife
when left on a countertop to soften, properly.
It is a solid prepared to go liquid,
whose melting point is the exact temperature
of your tongue.

Toast, when toasted perfectly, will cave under pressure —
cry-out, then collapse,
to tempt and warn us of its delicate insides.

I wash and iron your whitest shirts
and wear them when I'm feeling especially dirty
and naked underneath.

I'm not even sure why you like that so much,
but it makes me want to give you blowjobs
in your back seat,
in front of your ex-girlfriend's house.
The one that broke your heart into all those hungry,
crumbly, little pieces.

Tonight, I want you to come into my kitchen.
I'll cook you up something…
Extra long.
Extra slippery.

I'll feed you with my hands.
Hold the tangled strands high above your head—
Let them drop into your upturned, gaping mouth
and coil against the back of your throat.

Let the ends spill over your lips
so you have to slurp them in.

Let the sauce fly about the room.
Detonate burgundy-loaded fireworks,
to star-spangle and stain the ceiling.
Spatter and explode,
and rain down upon my face.

If you come tonight,
I'll find a way to make you want to stay
for toast.

Gluttony

Gluttony has no hands
to fold in prayer,
for giving thanks
or fingers to handle knives.

There is no patience
for bringing a bite
to your lips.

Your gut cannot be bothered
with the delicacy of forks.

Face and plate collide mid-air.
Mouth-slam, head-on,
a coital press into my porcelain.

Your forehead stained ripe-roma red.
Your hair is a rag mop.
Your clef chin is twisted siphon.
Your jowls— howling gutters.

There is no room for a drowning breath.
You cannot chew.
You only know how to swallow whole.

Your teeth are a wake of scavengers
damned to gnaw on scraps.
Tear at sinew.
Batter and bruise grizzle.
Your saliva blanches the bones.

Your tongue has no compass,
but it knows the corners and depths

of marrow canals.

Your throat has become a trench.
Your belly, a mass burial ground.

This is when winning wars
looks like victory
but feels most like regret.

3:55-4:00 AM

You've been partial to plaid, for years.
There are cobwebs in the corners of your ceiling.
You don't change your sheets very often—
But you fold clean laundry and match-up socks.
Five wire hangers, a laundry basket, and a folding chair
Contains your entire wardrobe.
You empty your trash and hold on to dead plants too long.
Your fan works.
Your clock radio is 5 minutes fast.
From this angle I can see your bathroom mirror.
You keep your toothbrush in a cup.
You cap the paste and use blue mouthwash.
You suffer from a heart murmur,
Or rabbit-chasing puppy dreams.
You don't wake up when your neighbor comes home drunk,
Or when I get up to leave.
This is everything I learned about you from 3:50-3:55 am,
      my time.

Your View

Of all the popcorn
ceilings in all the world, I
had to fall for yours.

Someone To Watch Over You

I like the way you wear demons
and tame most of my kind
with your fist.

And the way you startle
when my ghost-webs
come out to caress you in the night.

I'm the only one of us
who appreciates black-widow art.

When you sleep,
I drop down from a crack in the night
to tiptoe over your curves.

The first injection site is in a blue vein
that runs along the craving part of your neck.

Don't worry, I'm a professional,
after this you won't feel a thing.

The rise and fall of your breath is soothing.

Your skin is just the right amount of thin; it doesn't puncture
too easily.

It drives me wild that
even in your sleep
you can't help fighting back.

I too often make myself drunk on you.
I've no self-control

I'll stay until you become the death of me.

For the Love of Crime

We rode through the tri-colored suburban daylight
like it was the Mexican desert after midnight—
when no one was watching.

We were cowpokes aiming to wrangle hides.
Crossing the last border at high noon
to find us a barkeep and rile up the locals.

Knowing full well that drinking
with you always leads to planning,
and that planning leads to daring,
and daring leads to doing.

Guarantees are hard to come by,
so the next three rounds are on me.

Between us, we have a hand for safes
two left lazy eyes and a propensity for street fights.
A stomach for weakness and love for dynamite.

We weren't gunslingers per se—
but I'd been known to bring a few hand grenades
to ATM withdrawals just because you said you could always
be counted on for one last heist.

The only thing we ever agreed on was that nothing felt
more right than a perfect crime.

We stole more than we could get away with
and threw away more than we could afford to lose.

When you were shot down and the moon waxed on,
you begged for me to leave you behind
and let you bleed out in the street.

I couldn't do it.
The suburbs disapproved a fourth color.

I loved you like I love the desert,
like I love the night and crime.

I love you like I loved Mexico
when no one was watching.

The Laundromat

There was something about all those machines gathered in one place that fascinated us. Washers, driers, soap vending, a coin changer, and the last place in the city we knew of to play Galaga. Something that looked like a tampon dispenser hung askew and alone on the back wall. It had supplied something necessary at some point, but whatever it was, was apparently no longer needed by anyone. There'd never been a single complaint about it in the suggestion box.

Our mission that night was to use them all at once. Every machine. Laundry night usually meant hours of slapjack, grab ass, brain freeze and cherry Slurpee-stained lips. We had never thanked heaven for 7-11, but that was the time we decided it should begin as a tribute to everything that never closed and allowed us to get so many things done at once. Like that Donut shop on 4th, my bed, your refrigerator, and all that landmark, Laundromat light that let us know just how far from home we were.

This one had a level table for our cards and all our favorite brands; Talisman washers and driers, and Tide and Snuggle in those tiny boxes that made us feel like giants. We bought 20 of each and stuffed every slot with quarters. Two for Galaga, everything else cost a buck twenty-five.

We turned dials, selected washes and delicate cycles at random. Our palms grew raw from all those quarter slides. Then at 11 past 7 all the lids began to come down. You started at one end, me at the other; controlled chaos, we met somewhere in the middle— the no-man's land between washers and driers. We had both seen our share of trench warfare, but this was going to be diffcrent.

It began slowly like a few drizzles of rain looking to be a part of 15 minutes of fame. Mentioned on nightly news alongside pop stars, Storm Watches, and Doppler 7.

Oh the sound of it— freedom in the form of agitators and empty, out-of-control dryer spins. You know how much I love the empty spins, so you turned your back and let me alone for a minute with my favorite unbalanced dryer.

We called upon the full force of it— all that static electricity, all those simple machines living in belt and gear harmony. There was no fear. Nothing in that room was in danger of becoming any more self-aware. Only one washer ate our quarters and refused to run. We were relieved that no one would be called in to debug code or reboot systems. These were the kind of problems that could still be solved with wrenches and screwdrivers or just a good swift kick to the lid.

We channeled energy that could be mixed with our chi like the sweet forgiveness of Jameson's in our ginger ale. We held hands, as the earth shifted under our feet. The walls trembled sympathetically, and the plate glass windows threatened to jump their tracks. We'd all withstood so many dangerous quakes. So we convulsed with the freedom and precision of bake sale Jell-O molds. The fluorescent lighting pulsed, strained and fought the instinct to feel robbed of power, but not us; the power was ours. We could finally seal our fate as superheroes.

We'd invited the nannies, and the bartenders, the sailors and soldiers, the waiters and taxi drivers, the prostitutes and grad students, the washerless, the quarterless, and all homeless— the huddled masses longing for clean socks.

We spent an hour trying to convince the guy who beats everyone at chess in the park to come. He had lost part of one arm and most of his nose in the war. His clothes were always a mess. They all shook their heads figuring *it must be a ploy to sell washing machine timeshares*. It was hard for anyone to believe that getting clean could ever be free.

The first to arrive was a bus driver on his way home from work. He had to pass by no matter what. His uniform and a yellow stained undershirt shared a cycle with my tank top, mini-skirt, and your dad's old bowling shirt. Then the lady with her shopping cart of blankets and bags covered in pigeon droppings was granted a washer all to herself. The word had somehow passed through the streets. The place was packed, but no one knew what to do.

You stood in boxer-briefs and a civil servant's tan on top of the oversized dryer designed for sleeping bags and down comforters. What was left of your Cherry-Slurpee was held high above the crowd.

"Pick any washer," you proclaimed. "This is our night to finally feel clean again," but your words weren't enough. They were good words, they were, but most people still needed inspiration to strip down. So you dumped the remainder of your Slurpee on your head with all the grace of a door-to-door vacuum salesman, opened the lid to the closest washer, got down on your hands and knees, and immersed your beautiful cherry-stained head. The gangbangers stared in awe of you and your sud-fro. You looked ridiculous, but people cheered.

They began to take their clothes off and share machines. The soldiers and the unemployed tweaker teacher wore the same brand of underwear.

You told the waitresses and busboys to put their tips away. You said, "Your money is no good here." Sure, we could've taken all those quarters to Vegas, but we hated to gamble when there were so many things that still needed a guarantee.

Confiscating The Pencils

I want you solved like a crossword puzzle.
Each correct answer should describe you,
from your least significant thought
to your most profound belief.

Every fallacy you've bought a Scotch
for and every pornographic fantasy
you've sound tracked

Every thought you've ever had about me
and every insecurity you still hold about yourself.

What's a 4 letter word
for the 4 letter word
you've sworn off of?

If the downs and acrosses would sync up and band together,
I could finally make some sense of all of these questions
and uneducated guesses.

It may be foolish to believe that each truth
is essentially dependent on the others to be correct,
but I'll keep at it anyway.

I want you spelled out in black and white formation,
without any grey eraser smudges of corrections
to make me doubt all my previous deductions.

I want your truth.

The whole truth.
One answer
to answer them all.

It should come in the form of encircled
letters to be unscrambled at the end.

A secret code.

Lay naked with me on a Sunday morning.
I am confiscating the pencils.

Fill in every empty space.
Corroborate your answers.

Ink-stain my sheets and skin.

WE COULD HAVE BEEN HOT LIKE GIRL-ON GIRL

You Are Always Sending
Mixed Metaphors

On my birthday it was a bouquet
of dark-chocolate dipped, hypodermic needles
and I wondered if you'd become insulin dependent,
heroine addicted, or a death row inmate
with some conjugal visits to fill. Do I need Botox?
or have you reconsidered phlebotomy school?

For Christmas you sent a role of silver duct tape
and extra long zip-ties.
Had you detected leaks in my central nervous system?
Does your bum knee sense a hurricane coming?
Should I prepare for dirty bombs
or are you seeking an accomplice in a trophy-wife kidnapping?
Maybe it's just another way of telling me
to sit tight and shut up.

The jumper cables and caramel corn
could be a reminder of our S&M stay-cation.
Or perhaps the county fair is coming.
I remember how much burnt sugar smells like melting flesh.

Was the bowie knife and dinner fork
on Valentines Day for eating my own heart out?
Or is that your preferred silver pattern?
If so, I'd like to update the bridal registry.
I have listened to Space Oddity
12 times in a row, just to be safe.

A fire extinguisher, a bottle rocket,
and 9-volt batteries? You either still think I'm hot,
or else you remember how flammable my kitchen gets.
We both agree that my Fourth of July's

have always been too quiet.

It is now April. Only you would know
how much my tongue
misses the sting of anemone kisses.

We Broke Up Over a Colon

You didn't put the right parenthetical in its place
and I mistook what was supposed to be a smiley-face
for some kind of incomplete ultimatum.

I've apologized for all my typos and T-9 errors.
For the unintelligible, drunken, midnight-pleas,
and for frequenting bars with poor connectivity.

I'm even more regretful of the passive-aggressive
threats to switch cellular phone companies.
I'm sorry that I sometimes abbreviated your name
or didn't put enough x's or o's in my goodnight texts.

I wanted to be better for you, baby.
I wanted to write you epic love poems
140 characters at a time.

It seemed a way to keep things simple.
In the end it only castrated me
and frustrated you.

I'm sorry that our sexting landed your BlackBerry
in the toilet of the 7-11.
You shouldn't have been trying to masturbate in a public
restroom.

Please text me back.
I know, it was supposed to be
:)
XOXOXOX

I Speak Catastrophe

When the waitress asked how I wanted my eggs
I was relieved she could read my lips
and I didn't have to say the words, "over easy."

It didn't matter.
During lunch you'd texted "We're over"
and made it look a little too "easy."

When you called wanting to know what time
I was coming by to pick up my stuff
and drop off your key
you couldn't see me holding up
4 fingers and 2 thumbs.

To prevent further disaster,
I quacked 6 times and hung up.

A little after dusk, a half dozen ducks
are found dead at your door.
Limp-necked Kamikazes,
you called it an act of war
and refused to see me.

I take full responsibility.
Curses are my specialty.
Not even poultry is safe.

Yesterday my boss asked me to work
on Saturday. I considered letting him believe
I was coming down with the flu,
or that my great-uncle just died.
Instead, I played it safe
and signed the letters "O" and "K."

This morning I found myself achy and feverish,
at a funeral home in Tulsa, Oklahoma.

So now I carry a pad and paper everywhere.
I write down short answers to important questions,
and then erase them as fast as I can.

Except for tonight. When the waitress
asks what she can get me,
I will say your name as clearly as I can.

Late Riser

I. After Dawn

There are no worms left.
Not a single one.
I lay my head on a hot crust of Earth— later than ever.
Flying sucks.
I am never leaving the ground, again.
I will wait for the shade of a willow to come to me.
I am too tired and thirsty to find a drink.
There must be some drops of dew left on a blade of grass.
If I play dead, sooner or later
Something will crawl past and try to nibble on my leg.
That makes me early for lunch.

II. Before Dusk

Your song rained down through weeping branches.
Breaking silence and sound-tracking sunspots.
Exhaling my first breath of afterlife; I am revived.
This is the beginning of the end.
Lawless ripples have broken out along my spine.
My skin raises to be near you.
My hollow bones tremble beneath the micro-flutters of down.
I crave the comfort of your nest.
I fight it, but I can't turn off the honeysuckle.
Or the fertile wet gasp of pollen-covered seeds.
Nor my need for breakfast flesh…
You remind me to miss the sky.
Tomorrow you will be my reason to
Scratch in the dirt before sunrise.

Make-Up

Sex, just another
good reason to get into
bed with you, again

Sometimes You Have to Dive In

Even if it is to wreck yourself.
Even if it tumbles you raw and bloody.
Even if it tangles you up, drags you out, and tows you under.
Even if you must grow fins and gills to survive.

I will become crypto-mythological if I have to.
Your very own mermaidnado—
a spontaneous revolution.

At this rate—
by tomorrow
I will be all squirming fish
writhing on a hot bed of your coral.

You will be nothing but sucking arms,
ravenous mouth
and razor edged mercy.

Release me from the burn of this breathless misery,

Be the one who finally devours me.

Defying Physics

On the most unromantic of afternoons
you and I came together
like the gusts of wind off the Puget Sound
and the Tacoma Narrows Bridge.

We were complicit deadly chemistry,
set to self-destruct. Not by design—
but by our combined essence.

I'd been born into bondage
and was willing to lose limbs
for a few sweet reverberations of freedom.

You wore my rhythms like instinct
and committed seduction at a nuclear
and unconscionable level.

Tuning into me like hi-def, crystal-clear radio.
Filtering out every frequency apart from mine.

Your decisive search for harmonics
made for the slightest damping.
It was exquisitely timed foreplay
meant only to prolong the violence.

Your tones exhumed new depths
in me and caused my crests to sky-rise.
When your vibrato plied at my wavelengths
they spread themselves apart and wide.

Willing, but completely unprepared
to be ravaged and consumed
by the synergy of our mutually-exclusive,
ever-heartening amplitude

The resonance was fleeting.
It was our dissonance
that caused me to break so unevenly.

All that writhing and twisting
was just another way to escape
the structure that contained me.

Like Solomon's most misinterpreted song,
your timbre degraded and dissolved
during my demolition.

You were nothing more than a cunning linguist
armed with a lethal aero-elastic flutter.

I tried to defy physics and became life imitating
natural disaster—
an act of God.

I tore myself apart to become one with you,
to become something new.
If only there'd been a beautiful sound
to crumble into.

Dream Up A Downpour
And Wake A Puddle

I already begrudge this bed and the walls that separate us. The hands buried in my panties are too familiar. They try to mimic yours. This body both longs and refuses to be pandered to. It knows the weight of you. Your specific gravity. Your density. Your unplanned rhythm. The unevenness of your breath. I am thankful we never made it to your bed. The sting of skin ground away by rocky shore is a comfort. The race for pleasure to triumph over pain is sorely missed. The bruises and strained muscles of spreading open to you are painfully fresh. I have toyed with each one. Fingering tendons to remind myself of the bones that hammered mine. Testing inflictions. Reviving ache. Pinching the pinkest places between jagged nails to remind them of your teeth. It is no use. I cannot reincarnate you. I cannot fool myself. I lay alone, a puddle. Eyes closed. Incomplete. Unsatisfied. Unashamed. Thankful for the pain you left behind. It is the only thing this body will pretend to believe today.

Pretending You Are Here

That's your cup of tea
full of sugar and milk.
You don't laugh so much
or eat the cake on your plate.

You just look at me
wanting me to be quiet,
so we can kiss.

I wish I could tell you
how much I hate being alone,
how often I choose to be,
and how often I regret it.

I'm a hopeless addict
for the imaginary you.

I've memorized the way
sighs escape,
and the shape
my face takes,
every time
you appear
across a linen tablecloth.

Drowning In Your Blue

My pockets are so full of your blue
it is seeping through the seams of my jeans
and running down my legs.

I need a mop.

You have made a mockery of rain gutters
staining the rafters, and dissolving the sheetrock,
before heading out to become lost in the sea.

I want to grind the grime embedded under your nails
between my teeth.
I crave the taste of your clawing
and the collateral damage of your escape.
Your panic.
Your adrenaline and rebellion.
Your hard work, poor hygiene
and the sweat and skin of women
you'd swear you never loved
as much as you love me.

I swallowed the last eyelash
you left on my pillow,
that little piece of you went down
so easy, tasteless, and whole.
I can still feel it.

Trapped In Tadasana (Mountain)

I do not trust either foot.
There is always controversy
when a pelvis is shared.

I cannot release the cookie in my right hand.
I'll keep a balled up fist in the jar.
The left palm will never have a better plan.

"In" and "out" have too many different meanings now.
Lungs work independently.

I do not take sides.
Instead I inhale only when absolutely necessary
and exhale experimentally.

I let the cranial hemispheres argue over the directions.
None of the lobes can conceive of a final destination.
The ears will always disagree over what is too loud.
The tongue and ears will forever debate
the definition of sweet.

Love and fear have too many faces.
Do not stare.
Without notice every branch of hair can turn into hissing snake.

I cannot choose a foot, or a spot to place it.

Peace cannot survive.
For it is incapable of dividing itself evenly.

I pray for mercy from the wind and the rain.
I cannot become a tree.
I cannot reach for the sky.
I can only resist arrest.

THE MALIBU RUM BARBIE INTERVENTIONS

Rock Fight

We threw rocks at each other
unil we were bloody and battered.
You kissed me afterward
like it had been a good idea.

It was pretty cool.
The pain I inflicted on you
only made you want to hurt
me all the more.

That kind of party fuel
can get fucking intense.
It began like all of our skirmishes,
by me kicking up some dust,

and by you getting hit
somewhere around your chesticles.
One silent response led to another,
and it became a battle without duck or cover.

I'd never thrown so hard.
My shoulder dislocated.
Medium stones were best.
Palm-sized. Not too heavy to be swift.

There was a climax
where our aim became true
and vindictive.
We got past all the stinging, biting,
and splatters of blood, too quickly.

There was something strangely sweet and sadistic
in all the mudslinging—

threats of knives
and obscene gestures.

Damn, your trash talk was dirty.
I've always loved it,
but today I believed every word.

As the rocks got bigger I started to get scared.
The rules had never been clearly defined.

I worried how it would end—
neither of us being quitters.
One good blow to the head
could decide it all.

Would that have been the end of the game?
The end of me, the end of you,
or just another end of *us*?

If you'd gone down unconscious
I would have stood over you
with something formidable in my hand.
Palm-sized and swift.

We both know you'd do the same.

The Road Tripped

And you can't remember life before Street Pilots
and Google maps. My Rand McNally folding skills
have become obsolete.

What should I do with all these Thomas Guides?
Will we ever again have coffee with your name
misspelled on my cup?

Let's skip the coffee.
Instead, just pour a little of your Irish
directly into my mouth
and let's hit the road without so much as a compass.
That will allow me some space to unpack our past.

Our first kiss developmentally disabled me.
I became Malibu Rum Barbie,
and you were my porn star Ken.
I loved our dream townhouse
full of pink-plasticine bondage
and good old-fashioned, dry humping.
It predated the invention
of the refractory period.

But we can't ever go back because your anatomical parts
have a few better features than Ken's.
And, progress for progress' sake made us forget
that we didn't need anything in the first place.

You know we could have been hot like girl-on-girl
in my lip-gloss-stained, convertible Corvette.

But there wasn't enough appreciation
for good hair days
or attention to the art of man-scaping.

There were too many butterfly tramp-stamp
flirtations, and not enough hard-core,
grey-matter courting.

Never enough schoolyard honesty,
and too much back-alley fucking around.

Too much sorrow drowning under gas-lamp city nights.
Not enough tongueless kissing in suburban daylight.

We took too many flying ninja drugs
and couldn't maintain our Ginsu-knife love.

I've re-written all of our memories
to accommodate my lack of boundaries.

I can't stop blaming myself.
I am the black night sentenced to chase the sun.

The Summer You Left Me Without Any Respect

Aretha's Gold was the only thing that came from the cassette
player on the nightstand next to the bed. I'd listened, half
asleep to Side B more than a dozen times a day for three hot,
sad, sweaty months. It's only by coincidence that "Respect"
is on Side A.

Some moods are too low for changing sides or fast-forwarding
tapes. There isn't a song on that album that didn't rub
my broken bosom into a chocolate-whisky stained face.
No motivation was found for picking through un-alphabetized
shoebox collections.

Besides, I couldn't abandon Aretha when she needed me most.
The newspapers had piled up in a "do not disturb" trench.
I was fine only eating cereal without any milk, as long
as there was still tap water to wash it down.

I developed a new form of astrology based on constellations
that had formed in the popcorn of the acoustic ceiling.
My Jupiter is conjunct his mid-heaven. His moon
is in direct opposition to the cobwebs of my broken rotary fan.
It's no wonder; we've been doomed since birth.

I had long talks with her. I told her to forget him because no
man was worth that kind of pain. She was the Queen of Soul,
for God's sake, but nothing I said changed anything.

She just kept on singing our same sad memories. The tape took
me to the first of October. As the dew point achieved a record
low and the smog levels reached a record high. The cellophane
got tangled up in the spindles and Chain of Fools snapped in
two.

Solitude

I've taken to chewing on the wires
and the edges of the furniture.
The coffee tables, ottoman legs and headboards
have been reduced to mounds
of sawdust and wood chips.

Any lifted corners of wallpaper begged
to be liberated from the stucco.
Ragged strips of floral prints and pinstripes litter the hallways,
kitchen linoleum, and formal dining room.

I've dismantled appliances
with my only Phillips screw driver.
I don't own a flathead or anything metric.
In those cases, I've painstakingly used my teeth
and what was left of the nail on my left ring finger.
It's the only one that hasn't been chewed down to the bed.

I have removed every white feather
from the mattresses one at a time
and store them in the tub upstairs
where I take white downy baths
every Saturday night.

When pried away from the walls
with a curved claw hammer
the baseboards sound-off like rapid gunfire.

Dissecting all the light bulbs—
removing the filaments, wires, and stems
took three and a half days.

The way the invisible gases ignite
gives me a rush every time.

I throw the clear globes like hand grenades
at willow branches to drive the beady-eyed crows,
feral-cats and patent leathered parishioners from the yard.

Every page from The Holy Bible
and the white pages was admired
then individually torn from their spines.
I did my best not to recognize a single name.

I'm working on a novel about the science
of getting away with murder.

The first draft is written in blood.
Chapter one begins in the entryway.

As soon as my strength returns
Chapter two will continue
on the downstairs powder room mirror.

I haven't decided where the story will go.
But no matter what it should definitely end
in the cellar with a knife.

First Aide

You are bleeding to death.
Don't panic. I'm fairly qualified.
I've taken first aid.
I know everything there is to know about emergency-scene
management, when to call 911, and tick removal.

My high school health/gym teacher called me
"Hypocritically Gifted."
I still carry the 2nd semester report card in my purse—
if you care to see it.

Now just relax, I'm going to apply some pressure
to slow the blood loss.
You see I understand the differences between contusions
and abrasions and that being fractured
is the same as being broken.

I won't bore you with all the things I've learned
about head traumas and heart attacks.
But did you know that the first step in treating a burn
is to stop the burning?

God, I miss that class.
I can clearly recall the taste of the CPR dummy's lips,
vinyl laced with alcohol.
He was my dream man.
Sterilized and built to last.
I loved the way his chest plate popped in and out of place,
no matter how hard I compressed or pounded.

But what I remember most of all —
was the desire to utilize all my newly gained skills
and insight. I was done with my training
and wanted to use it on someone with a life on the line.

I wanted a victim.

I wanted to administer some cardiopulmonary resuscitations.

I carried a kit with me everywhere I went.
Triangle bandages, tweezers, sterile gauze
and my favorite triple-strength antibiotic cream —
the good stuff.

But years went by and no one needed
so much as a band-aid on my watch.
Everything had been left unopened beyond its expiration date.
Things began to yellow.
That's when I lost confidence.
The mere thought of blood or bones piercing skin
made me queasy.
What if I panicked and mistook a heart palpitation
for a psychotic break?

All it took was a good old-fashioned flesh wound,
not unlike your own, to get me back into the game.

As it turns out, I stay collected in the face of pain.
Stepford Wife calm before the storm.
Infuriatingly serene.

Of course, I'm not as good at it as I once thought
I'd be, but it's all I've ever wanted to do.

Sometimes, it feels as if there are more wounds
to clean than there is time to heal.

You are one of many who have depended
on me to prevent a bleed-out.
You must know that if I let go,
sooner or later, you'll have to, too.

Why do you look so disappointed by my stoic disposition?
I apologize. I assumed you wanted confident composure
while I applied the tourniquet.

You act as if you want me to panic and forgo
all my instincts and training.
You'd rather I'd flee the scene in fear and shame,
and leave you alone with your pain.
You want to be just another CPR dummy
whose chest plate always pops back into place—
no matter how hard I compress or pound.

Sorry, but I am a hand holder and a brow wiper.
I'm compelled to kiss every kind of hurt
until you can't feel a thing.

To be honest, things don't look so good for you.
I promise to do what I can.
I'll say all the right things.
I'll suggest deep breaths.
We'll say a prayer—
the kind that you like.
And then, I'll try to make you smile.

Go ahead and look up my skirt
if it helps to distract you from what I am about to do.
Whatever will get you to stop thinking about all that will be lost
when I'm finished mending you.

Before long the hemorrhaging will seize.
The pain will be gone
and you will have barely missed the severance.

Sometimes, even I forget that first aid
can't save everything.

Disembodied

I'll scratch your phantom
limb. I remember it much
better than you do.

I've Fixed Everything

I've burned all of our clothes.
Except for the ones you are wearing,
so hand them over; I've reserved a little gasoline.

My photographic memories and medications
along with your VHS tapes and all of our bills
made for great kindling.

I wish you'd have been here to revel in the boom.
The blaze: 451 degrees of porn and circumstance
singed my eyebrows and melted my bangs.

Once the reek of burning carbon and sulfur cleared,
the smell of freedom overcame my need for air.

The paperback novels cried arson
and refused to go down easy.
I was glad to be rid of the reference materials.
The dictionaries, Roget's Thesaurus, the 1964
Encyclopedia Britannica's, and the DSM-iv.

It was all hardbound historical fiction
that did nothing but put limits on our words,
arbitrarily label my mood swings,
and make that billing specialist at the ER
look like a miracle worker.

Your mother's only AA coin,
our large appliances, and a small fortune
in electronics had a deeper calling.
They have all been enlisted in the Salvation Army.

You will be proud to know that my self-portraits

and dressmaker's bust, along with your drum kit
and pool cue became performance art today —
having the ride of their life roped
to the top of a `72 Ford F150,
with 6 tons of our neighbor's barely-used,
warehouse house-wares bound for Tijuana.

I opened all the doors and every window,
but it wasn't enough.
The walls and the roof had to come down.
They'd been obstructing our view for too long.

Now we'll never miss another meteor shower.
Neither the Leonid nor the Perseid.
I know how much you still regret
the night we were having sex
and missed Halley's comet.

Now, we will know all of the phases
of the moon, first-hand.
We will feel the full brunt of its pull.
We'll drink to every bloody Tequila Sunrise
and wake to every Virgin Mary sunset.

I've fixed everything.
We are finally free to feel free again.

From Mark, To Shill, To Master

You and I share the world's record
for the longest running game of 3 Card Monte,
but in all police line-ups, rain, and frostbite
I've lost track of who was supposed to be conning whom.

I've mastered the art of the Mexican Turnover
but till get lost in your throw.

You've quit using the Queen of Hearts.
She makes marks feel uneasy.
You prefer the Ace of Spades.
Because everyone knows
If you wanna bury a whale ya gotta bring big shovel.

You've taught me that some will,
some won't, so what; pick their pocket just in case.

And that there's not much difference
between a cardboard box and a boardroom table.

Except the former has the advantage
of being folded up easier. You could pack up your game
and be 7 blocks away in 11 seconds flat.

We both lament that good shills aren't easier to come by.
Your "Rolex" watches skip the 1 o'clock hour, twice a day,
every other day.
You are perpetually falling back
and have developed tendonitis
from all the years of shuffling and winding.

My "Gucci" handbags all have slits in their lining
and smell like patchouli.
If anyone asks—

they fell off the back of an incense truck.

We've had price wars over bootleg DVD's
and turf wars over alley's and made peace and love
behind dumpsters.

I was the one who called the cops on you for public urination,
but only because you sold my only umbrella
while I was in line for the bathroom.

You still bring me free coffee from the shelter,
and I give you Vicoden prescribed for my dead grandmother.

You are little more than a swindler and a thief,
but I don't mind; you've taught me how to cheat the best liars.

No One Gives Good Prophesy Anymore

I am writing this because molehills don't have ears.
Mountains, they don't ever listen.

And, volcanoes—
pre, post, and mid-eruption--
hear nothing over the sound of their own roar.

Dabbling in God's rock and roll pyrotechnics
deafens us all to the screaming.

We cannot even hear our own.

Not the ones crying out in womb-gripping terror.
Nor the ones melting in flesh-frying pain,
Not even the one lost in the mind-blowing glory.

On her knees,
hands in prayer,
in the throws of rapture,

Praising her God
for his second coming
and excellent timing.

Who Are You Repenting For?

I come to you
having been puked
from the gut of a giant fish.

A skinless grape,
partially digested,
wall-to-wall ulcerations.

A single layer of sinew holds
the trembling jelly
and all that I am, together.

I come to you washed up,
freshly cauterized by the sea.
Opaque and hairless,
a glorious ghost
A miracle.
Your personal walking sacrament.

You refuse me shelter
then condemn me for my bloodstains
left on the shore.

You recognize the glory in my eyes
but neglect every grace and solace
unconditionally offered to you.

I come to you with ultimatums
and virgin sacrifices,
circumcisions, fire, and brimstone.

For that you drop to your knees and repent.
I never intended to be your prophet.
False or not, you forced me to.

Life is a Kaleidoscope

A circle of mirrors.
An endless reflection of color and light.
Break it open and dump out the guts.
Segregate them by shape and hue.
Stack the mirrors and line up their edges.
Discard the cracked and jagged.
Take stock in what isn't broken.
Update the inventory to account for—
Exponentially growing, negligible losses.
Isolate and analyze the materials using radiocarbon dating.
Examine each under a microscope.
Send a control group to Mars and observe it via satellite.
Offer the rest a drink of Windex.
Then just wait —
Sooner or later the mirrors will incriminate the glass.
Once they all plead the Fifth
Have the usual suspects held over for questioning.
Miranda rights and attorney privileges don't apply.
Tamper with evidence.
Threaten the justice of a jury comprised of dull peers.
Get them to sign a refracted confession and
Sign a multi-faceted peace treaty.
Sentence them to bell jar community service.
Wax-on, wax-off job training.
Insist on the completion of at least 7 out of the 11 steps.
Have them play tic-tac-toe
Once they actualize the futility of thermonuclear codependence
Insist they memorize the Serenity Prayer.
Teach them to meditate, mediate and medicate, as needed.
Let the beads believe they can grow up to be anything.
Rosary, Tesbih, Japa Mala or New Orleans flash-worthy.
If they see God— maybe He can explain
Why a telescope maker turned the universe in on itself.
Or why the time-traveler always insists on dying

In his own time, next to his favorite wife.
And why moon-walkers return to Canaveral
Without ever attempting to fly.

From The Girl On the Mountain—
To The Boy In The Sea

I huck black stones at the red rooftops
of your blue town, below. Hoping to hit yours
and wake you from your flightless, yellow sleep.

To knock you off your righteous green path
of perpetually fleeting success,
and to remind you that I still exist in 3-D,
Technicolor and stereo surround sound.

Your disappointed father
said you were born to be a white warrior.
Your proud mother
said you were a peaceful brown boy.
Your brothers have become violet kings
using your battle plans.

You chose to live for me
and the sea.
By your gut.
Upside down.
Underwater.
Seated in your capsized boat,
Using kites to fish silver-gulls
and shallow breaths
from a grenadine and orange juice sky.

Now, you spend all your time
scheduling sobriety,
defying DUI decimal logic,
undesignating drivers
and eluding intervention
by turning bottles into impotent sea glass.

I sit upon this green mountain.
A lone grey victor,
congratulating my feet on their triumph.
Drunk on darkness.
High on altitude.
Placid on platitudes.
Toasting technicalities.
Huzzah for hollow victories.

I've done nothing, except what you won't.
I've faced the pain and ignored the naysayers.
I've trusted my feet and taken the required number of steps.
I've forgiven the mountains that can't climb themselves.

The pink shoes I wore were meant for deep sea diving.
The trail did not care.
The white dress I wore was meant for wedding cake cutting.
The trees did not object.
The moonlight here demands a little leg and informality.
I give it what it wants and sit naked on the summit
with bare feet dangling in open air.

It gets lonely up here.
My lungs are dry.
My words are orange cedar dust.
My lips are sealed with amber tree sap.
But I still think you would like it.
There is music all the time.
It is inhaled through ears and exhaled through eyes.

You were wrong.
The stars haven't been tooled into a leather sky
as God's last-ditch, random act of regret.

Each one has a solid 500-billion-year plan.

You can't hear them, but the constellations
constantly make fun of you and laugh
at your disappointment in yourself.

I call down to you and beg for you to sing
the other half of your favorite drinking song.
Only the echoes of my own black voice
have returned to me.
They bounce off the red rooftops of your blue town.

I miss living below green sea level near you.
I miss your voice.
I miss your echo.
I have not given up.
You will get curious.

You must have heard the songs on nights
when brown liquids have run low
and yellow dreams never come.

I will always be waiting for you.
I know you will have to climb this mountain
if you ever want to see the view
your soundtrack was written for.

Your Ship Is Nearly Out Of Sight

On a clear day you would disappear slowly.
Today the air is thick with life.

Yet you appear farther away than ever
and you have only just left.

The Sun and all the things that had made you clear to me
have been dispersed amongst five winds.

I would keep blowing you kisses
but I don't want to fill your sails
any more than I already have.

Each one has pushed you farther
beyond my breath's reach.

The horizon can't hide you,
but you will follow it to a place
where I will not be able to see you.

Maybe to a place
from which you can never return.

GETTING OUR AFFAIRS IN ORBIT

Dear Rocketman

I know you feel alone.
For we are farther apart
than any two humans
have ever been.

Science may never know
how far love can go,
how long it can last,
or the speed it travels,
but I am always with you.

We co-exist in blurry flux.
Our electrons are constantly getting it on
in an alternate universe.

You feel me when I put your face to my needs.
When I break open and apart
just to help myself to sleep.

I want to know you.
Your books Apocrypha.
Your shredded documents.
Your wet nightmares.
All of your high and dry dirty laundry.
Tell me everything.
Rocketman,
I am here.

Tonguenastics

Remember my tongue tricks?
The ones that coil up on themselves;
Proof that recessive genes can become dominant.
I cross-train daily.
Ready. Set. Go.
En guard-- don your safety gear.
I've learned to filibuster in Sanskrit.
I've perfected pins, escapes, and reversals.
My static apnea is 7 minutes 11 seconds. Beat that.
I practice Zen and the art of the well-timed chokehold.
I've tested the limits of unnecessary roughness,
And play both harmonica and kazoo.
I am the ball and the goal.
I'm done with training videos
And impotent, Sci-fi, fantasy flicks.
Bring on the triple-x fucking reality.
I will suck out every ounce of pulpy fiction.
Simulations miss the nuances.
They can't train me for grace or teach attention to detail.
I want raw, hands-on, practical, real-world applications.
The fuel of an opponent's sweat.
Skinned knees, scarred backbones,
And carpet-fiber burned into flesh.
I want to learn to improvise, create suspense—
and hang on anticipation.
Test my tongue.
Game on.
I am ready to take one for the team.

Space Station Distress Signals

I broke orbit.
Now, I am alien.
An invader from an unknown world.

Out here, I am considered dangerous until dead.
Not worthy of mercy.
Doubled over with loneliness
I'd die to be remembered and live only to avoid death.

My want of you is not enough.
I am only a doorstop in a forgotten rear exit.
You are an escape hatch for the stars.

This is *not* tantric—
This is a bread and water suicide pact.
This is not the study of love or the practice of making it.

This is a self-tied straightjacket.

A dirty-needle Hail Mary—Oh, God.

Amen.

I make a mental note of what still glistens
in the ever-present night.
Daylight is a memory I am still learning to forget.
I am learning not to miss.
Learning to live without, and make do.

Climaxing under artificial light feels clinical
and over-calculated.
It is rushed choreography sorted out in obscene silence.

In the end, we all finish alone—

No matter how many faces we conjure
when our eyes are closed.

Like tight slot machine spin downs with curved pay-lines.
Round and round the faces go,
until mercifully you trip my lights fantastic.

Winner! Winner!
Finger licking dinner.

My touch alone isn't lethal enough for either of us.

God, bring to me the tentacles of beasts.
The tendrils of monsters hiding in the deep.
If not, I will drown in the sea of space.
There must be something out there with serrated teeth,
locking jaws, and talon feet.

Let it smell my hunger and taste my cravings.
Let it gravitate into my forgotten nightmares
of chained limbs and severed skin.

Bring to me certainty. Make it as final as death.
There is no point in holding onto a breath.
There is no surface to rise to, only infinity to fall into.

Space

The space between us
is the sculpture I cannot
stop overworking

I woke to wet silence

A kiss pressed
to my cheek.

Its breath lingered
between my breasts
and dampened
the sheets.

You had carved
the shape of a heart
and our initials
into the fogged-up
windowpane.

Its stain serves
no other purpose
than to return
on rainy days
when memories
hurt most.

Our chance to be great
has come and gone.

It's no use.
We can't survive
on my clouded memory
alone.

DIGGING YOU UP AND HOLDING YOU AGAIN

Letting Go

I held on too long, lizard tail.
Monarch wing stained fingertips, too strong.

The hair of your chinny-chin-chin
was still attached when I slipped it into my
mother's bear-trap locket.

You couldn't gnaw yourself away fast enough.
I couldn't strangle you slow enough.

I only half considered burying
what was left of you half alive.

I was Komodo dragon committed
to letting you claw your way out.

I swear.

But after my locked jaw, pit-bull shake farewell,
you couldn't muster a single tear.

I left the back door ajar.
It is no wonder you didn't survive the night.

You took off without your ability to flourish, fly, or kiss.

I set you free for nothing.

Now I'll never know
if you were meant to be mine.

Reversing Rigor Mortis

By all accounts you are dead.
I rolled you onto your side
and propped you up with pillows.

One cool arm under my neck,
the other is pulled over my shoulder.
My cheek settled into your perfectly still chest.
For a moment I was certain warmth was returning to you.

It was your final joke.
The temperature of my blood was dropping to match yours.
As if trying to catch you,
wherever you were going. wherever you had gone.
Somewhere or anywhere.
Even if it felt like death.

Your arms drew me in and grew unbearably heavy.
Alone in my labored wet breath.
Trapped by the immovable.
Panic came next.
Who knew rigor mortis would feel so much like love?

Parade

A flag flies wild at half-staff—
I can't help but think of the strangers
who left us all behind.

But I can't stop there;
every wrongful death parades
along my mental block.

There are beautiful, bikini-clad bodies
waving from atop '60 something, convertible,
wide-whales with razor-sharp tailfins.

Soldiers and war children
sail down the boulevard
side-by side on wooden farm wagons
converted into cotton candy floats.

All of them waving prosthetic legs
in the air like they couldn't care more.

My mother Harlem shuffles
while pushing her own wheelchair,
under a shower of ticker tape

The sun beats down.
The day becomes a wool suit.
I can't wait to leave, but I haven't seen you yet.

I worry you might have snuck-by
when the drum line played Amazing Grace.

Dry and cracked, my lips split
and buckle like sidewalks.
My mouth waters for whatever poison took you.

I do not pray for merciful death.
I've only brought self-inflicted knife twists,
hidden deep, in a less than lethal place.

A mosquito buzzes near my ear.
I slap without thinking.
That is when I recognize your smear
on my hand.

Anniversary Traditions

The soil outside our window
is loose and fresh.
The mound of earth could be mistaken as future bed
for daffodil bulbs or sweet baby lettuce.

I try not to dig you up as often as I used to.
Perhaps it is a mistake to always re-bury
you with your letters.

One for every week you wandered the sea.
One for every holiday you spent celebrating yourself.
And one for every birthday I mourned being alive without you.

Your letters still sound more hopeful
than birth announcements.
As poignant as the first time I feared breaking their seal.

Your saliva has always been the glue
that held me together.

I welcome the paper cuts.
I treasure the calluses from the splintered shovel handle.
The dirt under my nails tastes like bourbon
mixed with your brand of shaving cream.

I am forever curious about the state
of your decomposition.
Is your hair still growing?
Have any of your fillings fallen out?

Will your skin still reflect the moon's
light on a warm summer night.

The letters remind me of how things still are

I can never celebrate our birth
without mourning our death—

without digging you up
and holding you again.

Ward G2

My return was more than voluntary. I am committed to regaining some of my misunderstood sanity. A 72-hour hold certainly couldn't hurt. I keep my bunk free of clutter and stick to a routine that includes kitchen duty. Cooking and cleaning, anything to avoid a day of hard labor in direct-sun. This work they give us, especially the physical, is good for the constitution. A little vitamin D is essential for reversing a depleting dopamine problem. The simple tasks of washing dishes, chopping vegetables, and taking out the garbage keeps hands relatively blood free. I am happy here amongst the loons, the roadrunners, and the squirrels. Stirring boiling pots and ladling thick stew onto plates held out by the most blissful looking faces I've ever seen. It really is all about the people. Having me around somehow makes them feel saner. It is the least I can do for my kind.

Dismantling a Shrine

Remove the pedestal.
Un-light the candles.
Reincarnate the wax.
Blow ashes back into incense.
Pencil in a toothbrush mustache.
Re-attach the daisy petals to their stems.
Bury the lock of hair to prevent birds from building nests.
Return the marble to its place in the quarry.
Action figures should be tarred and feathered,
Drawn and quartered. Heart and lungs removed,
And placed on a 75%-off table.
Have the autographs de-authenticated.
Let the albums warp in direct sun.
Baptize the poetry in acid.
Release the gimp.
Eat the chocolate.
Drown the cat.
Drink the wine.
Uncross yourself.
Reverse genuflect.
Revoke every prayer.
Walk backwards from the room.
Leave a trail of fuel.
Light a match.
Begin again.

To The Four-Chambered Congress
In My Rib Cage

I am resigning my post as Poet Laureate to
The Sovereign Nation of Broken and Lonely.
Alert C-Span and cancel my annual speech
on the state of our union.
My duties were too minimal
and I've temporarily lost control of my polarities.

I have cleared out my desk, boxed up the heart
and highlighted the scars.
Have it delivered to my successor as a reminder
not to dwell on metaphors for too long.

Let this body be nothing more than a vehicle
for transporting my head.
Heart-optional positions can't be that hard to come by.

I feel most qualified to be an undertaker.
There will be no danger of growing intellectually involved
with any more horizontal, brain-dead stiffs.

I'd make an excellent traveling salesman,
throwing dirt clods in doorways
to get the lady of the house
to let me bring my small appliances in.
Without reservation I would guarantee my attachments
to reach into the deepest of crevices
and squeeze into tightest of spaces.
They will suck away problems she never knew she had.

If I were an accountant, I'd be one to the stars
and think of nothing more complicated than spreadsheets,
how to write-off medicinal lap dances,

and depreciate incriminating liquid-assets.

I'd be willing to de-down geese for a comforter company
or slip fortunes between cracks
in a Chinese cookie factory.

I could become the voice over the P.A. at the DMV.
B7 -- Window number 11 is now available.

Or, I could open a Hooters
just outside the Braille institute.

I've always wanted to be a zookeeper.
Just once allow me to feed the monkeys
without regard for freedom, free love, or inbreeding.

If I become a bailiff I'll be all handcuffs and hard-ass.
Holding up Bibles without any guilt.
Raise your right hand and swear to tell the truth,
your half-truth, or as much of it as you can still bear—
so help you God.

Relax, I doubt He cares,
and the truth no longer matters to me.

I am ready to be a migrant farm worker.
There will be no more pity for things like volunteers
and rotting fruit.

Twenty-Seven Views
Of A Rolling Stone
"How does it feel?"-Bob Dylan

1.

Desert floor, mountain road,
river bottom and bed—all the homes she doesn't
remember to miss.

2.

Was once part molten and swam with lava.

3.

Living at the shore now.
Never been better. Can't send a postcard
or fathom wishing you were here.

4.

Lacks muscle memory
and shame for being complicit
in starting the first forest fire.

5.

Harbors no regret for the avalanches
she's started, or has been a part of.,
and yes, she is absolutely the type
who'd go over a cliff just because
everyone else was doing it.

6.

Never got any press for preventing
the landslide in '89 or the Tsunami last month.

7.
Sees no crime in cavorting with snowballs,
gang bangers, hurricanes, rabbit hunters,
hailstorms, preschoolers, or polar ice caps.

8.
She's confronted plate glass
and has had more than her fair share
of chance encounters with rear-passenger side windows.

9.
Was kicked along sidewalks
for a record of 66 consecutive blocks.

10.
Has been laid on numerous tracks,
and ridden in cattle cars
from Vancouver to Cabo San Lucas.

11.
She's been swallowed by a brown-nosed calf
and has been carried by an eagle to shore up a nest.

12.
Shared denim pockets with bottle caps,
condoms, cigarette lighters, silver bullets,
and shiny black night crawlers

13.
Survived spin cycles
and being lodged in a lint filter.

14.
In her younger days she had moves like Jagger.
Razor enough to be mistaken for a shark's tooth.

15.
She's been lottery prize and has been held
by the heavy hand of justice.

16.
Once moonlighted as a raccoon's breakfast table
and worked the swing shift as an otter hammer.

17.
She split logs for a barn raising in Upstate New York.
And was the cornerstone of the first Baptist church
to ever go up in smoke.

18.
Was part of a convoy's final leg delivering
10-tons of Detroit muscle.
Handle: Stone Cold Fox.

19.
She's been a paperweight, doorstop
and Zen garden scribe.

20.
One of a million doppelgangers
scattered all over the Universe.
Note: Get's lost in crowds easily.

21.
A chip off the old block.
Her brothers and sisters
never recognize each other.

22.
She doesn't have an 800-number,
or cell. Doesn't care if no one calls.

23.
She worked as a slippery
foothold in sleep-away camp's stream.
Challenging balance
and twisting weak ankles for a month of summers.

24.
More than a decade she wasted time living
in a landfill amongst illegally
dumped, bio-hazardous waste
and never noticed.

25.
God, it was a relief when
she finally gave up the moss.

26.
Shatter resistant

27.
Smooth. Black. Oval.

Oh, Mountain

Do not tempt me today.
You are surmountable.
Conquerable.
And no longer worthy
of my attention.

You are there.
Always due east, waiting,
even though I've asked you not to.

You know I have already prevailed.

You and your summit—
I know all 360 degrees
of its unobstructed view, by heart.

I know your deepest, darkest valleys
every well-worn trail,
faulty foothold,
and slippery, sodden, rockslide to the bottom
better than you do.

There is still time for you to run.

You may have risen from the Earth's core
and spewed molten lava
over my father's farmland
and its nursing mothers.

The fisherman's bare-chested
sons were boiled alive.

My sisters have been vaporized
by your breath.

But your anticipation of me
is wearing you down.
You lie in someone else's shadow now.

Before long you will be a smooth black river stone
I can hold in the palm of my hand,
kiss goodbye,
and skip across the sea.

ACKNOWLEDGMENTS

Thank you to Luke Salazar and Eric Morago for taking on the
momentous task of editing the majority of this book.
And, many thanks to my poetry family and friends for offering
editing suggestions, a shoulder to beat my head against,
or in some cases three fingers of Irish-whisky wisdom.
But mostly freedom to be as free as I need to be:
Ben Trigg, Steve Ramirez, Jaimes Palacio,
Derrick Brown, Andy Buell, Daniel McGinn,
and my Dirty Dozen Compadres,
Lori McGinn, G. Murray Thomas, Brendan Constantine
Joanne and Ed Baines
Alexander Benavides, Ken Schmidt, Phil and The Ugly Mug,
Deanne Brown, The SOCHS Families, Daisy Chain,
Ralph & Eleanor Moore,
Savanah Moore-Kondo, Harrison Moore-Kondo.
and most of all my love, Michael Kondo.

Raundi K. Moore-Kondo is convinced that the zombie apocalypse is a metaphor for poetry. Which explains her compulsion to want to infect everyone with it. This led her to develop *For The Love of Words Poetry & Creative Writing Workshops* for writers of all ages.

She has been previously published in *Don't Blame the Ugly Mug* on Tebot Bach, *Aim For The Head* on Write Bloody Press, *Lummox Vols. I and II,* and *Donut Touch Me* on Bank Heavy Press. She has been the Poet of the Month for Moon Tide Press, a Featured guest on KPFK's Poet's Café, and the winner of The Lightbulb Mouth Literary Adventure Part V.

Raundi has self-published an all-ages poetry anthology called *A Poet Is A Poet No Matter How Tall,* A Chapbook for Breast Cancer Awareness *The Hills Are Alive* and a full-length novel <u>The Revival</u>.

When she isn't pushing poetry on people she plays bass in the band *Daisy Chain*, is wife to Michael, and mom to Savanah and Harrison. She makes an excellent body-boarding, rollerblading, mountain biking and writing buddy. Hit her up at—
www.theloveofwords.com

Made in the USA
San Bernardino, CA
05 November 2014